The Coffee Shift

Perspectives, Cat Wisdom, and the Power of a Good Cup of Coffee

---

Beenie Mann

Good Spirit Publishing

The Coffee Shift: Perspectives, Cat Wisdom, and the Power of a Good Cup of Coffee

Copyright © 2025 by Beenie Mann

All rights reserved. No part of this book may be reproduced or transmitted in any form or by any means without written permission from the author. This includes reprints, excerpts, photocopying, recording, or any further means of reproducing text. Contact Sabine (Beenie) Mann through her website, www.BeenieMann.com

The material in this book is intended for education. It is not meant to take the place of diagnosis and treatment by a qualified medical practitioner or therapist. No guarantee of the effects of using the recommendations can be given, nor liability taken.

ISBN 978-1-963057-16-4

Printed in USA

Other books by Beenie Mann:

Happiness Matters: Unleash Your Superpower in 7 Easy Steps
Square Peg Round Hole
Mo-the Service Dog: Because Every Dog has a Purpose
Happiness Matters: You are NOT Alone!
WTF Do I Do Now???
The Ego Trap
Matters of Perspective: A Year of WTF Questions
and more…

Because life is better with coffee, cats, and a little chaos…

For every soul who's ever needed a fresh cup, a fresh start, and a reminder that you're not alone — may these pages bring you perspective, courage, and a smile when you need it most.

and…

To Gandalf and Zafira — for reminding me daily that naps are essential, curiosity is a superpower, and knocking things off the counter is an art form.

Acknowledgments

To say this book wouldn't exist without you is an understatement — it wouldn't even be a half-finished Google Doc with coffee stains on it.

First, to **my readers** — you're the reason I brew the words, pour them onto paper, and serve them with extra sass. You've laughed with me, cried with me, and occasionally sent me cat memes that are *way too accurate*. I am forever grateful.

To **my family and friends** — thank you for loving both Beenie *and* Sabine, even when we take turns hogging the microphone. Your patience, encouragement, and gentle "maybe you should have another coffee before hitting send" interventions have been priceless.

To **my cats, Gandalf and Zafira** — your contribution to this book has been… let's call it "enthusiastic." From deleting paragraphs by strolling across the keyboard to offering purr therapy during deadlines, you've reminded me that sometimes the best ideas happen when you step away and play with a string.

To **the coffee farmers, roasters, and baristas of the world** — you are the true unsung heroes. Without you, this book would have been titled *The Nap Shift*.

To **the Happiness Matters Foundation dream team** — you inspire me daily with your passion, commitment, and belief that hope and change are not just possible, but inevitable.

And finally, to **the part of me that healed** — Sabine, thank you for coming home. And to Beenie, thank you for never leaving. Together, we brewed something pretty darn special.

Table of Contents

Introduction: Before We Get Started… .... *vii*

Chapter 1: The Sock Dimension *1*

Chapter 2: The Latte of Life *7*

Chapter 3: GPS for the Soul *13*

Chapter 4: The Ego's Costume Party *21*

Chapter 5: Quantum Leap in Pajamas *27*

Chapter 6: Cats Don't Apologize *33*

Chapter 7: The 3 AM Brain Circus *39*

Chapter 8: GPS Recalculating… Again *45*

Chapter 9: The Gratitude Glitch *51*

Chapter 10: Sock Dimension, Part II: The Return of the Tupperware Lid *57*

Chapter 11: Laser Pointer Goals *63*

Chapter 12: The Universal Lost & Found *69*

Chapter 13: Cat Wisdom for Humans *75*

Chapter 14: The Cosmic Customer Service Line *81*

Chapter 15: The Art of the Strategic Nope *87*

Chapter 16: The Last Cup in the Pot *91*

Chapter 17: And Another Thing… *95*

About the Author *99*

Introduction: **Before We Get Started...**

(Or: How We Ended Up Here in the First Place)

So here's the thing — I didn't set out to write this book.

I mean, sure, I've written books before. I've shared my stories, my hard-earned wisdom, and the occasional sass bomb. But *this*? This started as a conversation... with myself.

Not in the "uh-oh, she's lost it" way — more like a dialogue between two parts of me: **Beenie** and **Sabine**.

Meet Beenie and Sabine

Sabine is my given name — the one I grew up with. But here's the thing: for a long time, "Sabine" reminded me of my messy, painful childhood. In 2009, when friends started calling me Beenie, it felt like a fresh start. Beenie was light, playful, full of possibility. I loved her energy so much that I happily tucked "Sabine" away.

Then, in 2023, something shifted. I had healed enough to let Sabine re-emerge — not as the wounded girl from my past, but as the wise, grounded version of myself who'd made it through. And here's the beautiful part: Beenie didn't go anywhere. She's still the spark, the humor, the sass. Sabine is the depth, the perspective, the steady anchor. Together, they make… well, me.

So in this book, when you see the back-and-forth, that's Beenie and Sabine in conversation. Two sides of the same coin — one cracking jokes, the other dropping truth bombs — both here to help you see life from a fresh perspective.

What You'll Find Here

- **True stories** — Some are funny, some are raw, some will make you wonder how I'm still allowed out in public.
- **Conversations** — Real back-and-forth between Beenie and Sabine, where the banter is half the fun and the wisdom sneaks in between the jokes.

- **Cat Corner** — Yes, the cats weigh in. No, they don't always stay on topic.
- **Mini wisdom bombs** — Quick truths you can scribble on a Post-it and stick to your fridge, mirror, or forehead (your call).
- **Dares** — Little challenges to nudge you into action, because reading is nice but living is better.

How This All Came Together

For years, I'd been collecting these little life moments — both mine and the ones people shared with me during sessions, coffee chats, and those 2 a.m. "life crisis" calls. I didn't know what to do with them until one day, I thought, *What if I just wrote them all down like I was talking to a friend?*

Spoiler: That's exactly what I did. No overcomplicated plan. No ten-step formula. Just me, the two halves of myself, a laptop, and a couple of cats who think keyboards are heated beds.

What I Hope You Get Out of This

I'm not here to tell you how to live your life. I'm here to remind you that you *get* to live it — and that every day is a chance to shift your perspective, even a little. You'll laugh, you might tear up, and you'll definitely get at least one piece of advice that makes you go, "Dang… I needed to hear that."

Beenie:
Ready?

Sabine:
Always. Let's brew this thing.

Chapter 1: **The Sock Dimension**

(Because life lessons hide in laundry baskets too.)

Beenie:

Sabine, we need to talk. My washing machine is clearly a portal to another dimension. I put in ten socks, and only nine come out. Every. Single. Time.

Sabine:

Ah, yes. You've discovered the *Sock Dimension* — a parallel universe where all the missing socks, pens, and Tupperware lids hang out sipping margaritas and swapping stories about how they escaped.

Beenie:

Figures. I bet they're living their best life, all matched up and hole-free, while I'm here rocking the "fashionably mismatched" look like I'm auditioning for a quirky indie film.

Sabine:

Well, at least you're *owning* the mismatched look. But the Sock Dimension isn't just a laundry phenomenon — it's a metaphor. It's where all the "missing pieces" of your life go. Lost opportunities, that one friendship that faded, your youthful metabolism, the extra patience you swore you'd have as an adult… they're all in there somewhere.

The Lesson in the Lint

Life's got its own version of the spin cycle, and sometimes things — and people — just disappear from our lives. Sometimes for a reason, sometimes without any clear explanation. You can spend your days obsessing over where the socks went (and maybe become that person in the laundry aisle whispering, *"I will find you"* to a pack of crew socks), or you can shrug, laugh, and focus on what's still in your drawer.

When you release your attachment to what's missing, you make space for what's coming. And who knows? Sometimes life sends you a new pair of socks you like even better — metaphorical *and* literal.

Beenie:
So basically, let the socks go?

Sabine:

Exactly. If they were meant for you, they wouldn't get stuck in someone else's spin cycle.

Story Time

When I was a kid, I had this stuffed bear. Loved that thing like it was my own child. Took it everywhere — family trips, the grocery store, even the doctor's office (where, in hindsight, it probably caught every germ known to mankind).

One day, poof — gone. I was devastated. I looked under the bed, in the backyard, even accused my brother of running a black-market teddy bear operation.

A few weeks later, my aunt gave me a brand-new stuffed animal. At first, I stubbornly refused to love it. But slowly, it became my new favorite — softer, cleaner, and a little less… drool-stained. Losing that bear hurt, but it made room for something better.

We've all got our "stuffed bear" moments — the job we didn't get, the relationship that ended, the opportunity that passed us by. Sometimes, the universe is just making space.

Mini Wisdom Bombs

- *Not every mystery needs solving. Some just need laughing at.*
- *If it's truly yours, it'll circle back.*
- *If it's gone, maybe it's clearing the shelf for something better.*

Beenie:
Okay, but what if the sock *was* my favorite? What if it's the *perfect* sock — you know, the one with just the right stretch and the cozy-but-not-suffocating cuff?

Sabine:
Then you honor its service, give it a proper send-off, and let it go with gratitude. Preferably without building a shrine in the laundry room.

The Emotional Sock Drawer
We all have emotional "sock drawers" — the mental spaces where we store the people, things, and dreams we've lost. Some of them are missing a

match. Some are worn thin. Some we keep "just in case" even though we know they'll never be quite right again.

The danger? We hold onto those mismatched pieces so tightly that we crowd out room for the new. Your life isn't a museum — it's a rotating wardrobe.

Beenie:
So, you're saying I should Marie Kondo my emotional sock drawer?

Sabine:
Exactly — but with more laughter and less pressure to fold things into perfect rectangles.

Cat Corner 🐾

Gandalf: "Humans panic over socks. I hide mine under the couch for *fun*."
Zafira: "Try losing a mouse toy mid-chase. That's betrayal."

Beenie's Dare
Think of one thing you've been stressing about losing — a thing, a relationship, an opportunity.

Today, decide to let it go. Bonus points if you can laugh while doing it.

(Extra credit if you tell someone about your "Sock Dimension" moment — laughter is contagious.)

Sabine's Brain Spark

If socks can live happily in the Sock Dimension without your supervision, maybe other parts of your life can too.

Closing Wink

So next time you lose a sock, smile. You've just contributed to the thriving population of the Sock Dimension — and who knows, maybe they'll send you a postcard. Or at least return that Tupperware lid you've been missing since 2017.

Chapter 2: **The Latte of Life**

(Mindset is the foam. Trust me on this.)

Beenie:
Sabine, I've decided coffee is the perfect metaphor for life.

Sabine:
Oh? And here I thought you just drank it to keep from biting people before 9 a.m.

Beenie:
That too. But seriously — you've got the base coffee, which is your circumstances, and then the foam... that's your mindset. You can have the most amazing coffee beans in the world, but if the foam's all flat and sad, the whole drink just feels... meh.

Sabine:
So basically, you're saying a bad mindset can ruin a perfectly good life?

Beenie:
Exactly. And on the flip side, even if your beans are a bit burnt — like maybe you're going through a

rough patch — if you whip up that foam just right, you can still make the experience smooth and enjoyable.

Foam First, Flavor Follows

Life doesn't start tasting better when everything's perfect. It starts tasting better when you decide to make it better. Foam isn't just decoration — it's presentation, texture, and that first sip experience. Your mindset works the same way.

I've seen people with "perfect" lives who can't enjoy a single sip because they're too focused on the temperature, the mug, the one bubble in the foam that's slightly off-center. And I've seen people going through storms, sipping their coffee in a chipped mug with a smile, because they know foam isn't forever — but joy can be.

Beenie:
So what's the trick to keeping my foam happy?

Sabine:
Gratitude, perspective, and a dash of not taking yourself too seriously.

Story Time

Years ago, I was in one of those "burnt bean" seasons. Everything felt over-extracted and bitter. One day, I stopped into this tiny coffee shop, and the barista — bless her caffeinated soul — handed me the prettiest latte I'd ever seen. Perfect little heart drawn in the foam.

I just stared at it for a moment. My life was still messy. The problems hadn't gone anywhere. But that foam? That tiny piece of beauty? It shifted something in me.

That's when I realized — we can't always control the beans, but we *can* control the foam.

Beenie:
So… we're all our own baristas?

Sabine:
Exactly. And some days, you might spill the milk or burn your tongue, but you keep making coffee anyway — because without it, you're just sitting in the kitchen staring at an empty mug.

Mindset Foam Art

Think of your mindset as the design you swirl into your foam:

- **Heart** = approaching life with love.
- **Leaf** = growth and learning.
- **Rosetta** = okay, that one's just to show off.

  The art isn't permanent — you drink it. But in that moment, it changes your experience entirely.

Mini Wisdom Bombs

- *Mindset is the foam — it's what hits your lips first.*
- *Your life's flavor comes from both the beans and how you serve it.*
- *Bitterness happens — sugar and foam are optional but powerful.*

Beenie:
But what if the foam's already flat? Like, I wake up and just feel "meh" before my feet even hit the floor?

Sabine:
Then you become your own barista reset button.

Change the mug. Add cinnamon. Play music while you make your coffee. Shake yourself out of autopilot. The foam will follow.

Cat Corner 🐾

Gandalf: "Foam is just fancy bubbles. I'd rather have cream."

Zafira: "I once stuck my face in foam. Regret. So much regret."

Beenie's Dare

Tomorrow morning, before you grab your coffee (or tea, or smoothie), decide how you're going to foam your day. One thing you'll do to lift your mindset *before* life has a chance to burn your beans.

Sabine's Brain Spark

Life is a series of sips. The foam doesn't last, but the way you savor it does.

Closing Wink

So the next time someone asks how you're doing, tell them, "Perfect foam today." And if they look at you funny, just smile — you've got your own latte of life brewing, and they're not ready for your recipe.

Chapter 3: **GPS for the Soul**

(Because "recalculating" is not a failure — it's a feature.)

Beenie:

Sabine, I swear my car's GPS has a personal vendetta against me. The other day, it told me to "make a legal U-turn" — on a street where the only "legal" part was the fact that I didn't get arrested for trying.

Sabine:

Well, maybe it's just trying to keep life exciting. Besides, GPSes are the perfect metaphor for life direction — we all think we're headed straight to our destination, and then, boom... road closed, detour, potholes the size of kiddie pools.

Beenie:

Don't forget the moments where it insists you've "arrived at your destination" but you're actually in front of a stranger's house wondering if they'll mind you parking in their driveway to eat your emergency snack stash.

Your Inner Navigation System

Here's the truth: You've got a GPS inside you. Call it intuition, soul compass, gut feeling — whatever makes you feel less like you're in a self-help seminar and more like you're tapping into your personal Google Maps.

The problem? We ignore it. We second-guess. We prefer the voice that sounds certain, even if it's taking us straight into a dead end.

Your soul GPS doesn't yell, "Turn left now!" with robotic urgency. It whispers. It nudges. Sometimes it just makes you *feel* like you should take a different road.

Beenie:
Okay, but what if my inner GPS is broken?

Sabine:
It's never broken. It might be recalculating because you've been ignoring it, or maybe you've been driving in circles because you're waiting for the perfect set of directions before you even start moving.

Story Time

For a while, I was convinced I was "supposed" to be a mortgage loan officer. I got licensed, dressed the part, learned the lingo — because that's what I thought a responsible, capable adult *should* do.

Except... I was miserable. I didn't close a single mortgage. Not one. Every day felt like slogging through wet cement in high heels. My enthusiasm flatlined somewhere between my hundredth cold call and my fiftieth awkward networking event.

Then came the morning of April 1st, 2018 — and no, the irony of April Fool's Day is not lost on me. I woke up, stared at myself in the mirror, and thought, *Oh, this is stupid! Why am I doing this? I'm miserable and just going through the motions.*

Right then and there, I decided I was done shoulding all over myself. No more living by other people's expectations. No more convincing myself that "responsible" and "soul-sucking" were the same thing. I made the decision, walked away, and didn't look back.

It didn't magically drop a perfectly drawn map in my lap, but it did flip my inner GPS from "off" to "navigating." And you know what? The detours since then have been way more interesting.

Recalculating Isn't Failure

Think about it: When your GPS says "recalculating," do you throw the thing out the window and declare you'll never drive again? No. You keep going — maybe slower, maybe more cautiously, but you keep moving.

In life, "recalculating" moments are just pivots. They're not proof that you messed up; they're proof that you're paying attention.

Beenie:
So, my wrong turns aren't actually wrong?

Sabine:
Exactly. They're scenic routes you didn't plan for — but that doesn't make them useless.

Signs You're Ignoring Your Inner GPS

- You keep asking everyone else for directions instead of checking in with yourself.
- You're more focused on *what if I get lost* than *what if I discover something amazing.*
- You're parked on the side of the road, waiting for 100% certainty before moving.

Mini Wisdom Bombs

- *You can't course-correct if you're not in motion.*
- *The map doesn't have every detail — but you don't need it to start the journey.*
- *Trust the recalculations. They're where the growth happens.*

Practical Soul GPS Tips

- **Check your coordinates regularly:** Pause and see if your current direction still feels right.
- **Don't be afraid of detours:** Sometimes they lead to the exact thing you didn't know you needed.

- **Remember the destination can change:** The goal you set five years ago might not be the goal you want now.

Beenie:

So basically, stop waiting for perfect clarity and just start driving?

Sabine:

Yup. And maybe pack snacks — spiritual and literal.

Cat Corner 🐾

Gandalf: "I always know where I'm going. Usually to the treat cupboard."

Zafira: "My GPS says nap now. It's never wrong."

Beenie's Dare

Think of one decision you've been stalling on because you're afraid it's the wrong turn. This week, take one step — any step — in that direction. Let the recalculating happen later if needed.

Sabine's Brain Spark

Your soul GPS never gets tired of you. You can ignore it for years, and the moment you listen, it simply says, "In 500 feet, turn left."

Closing Wink

So next time life says "recalculating," smile. You're not lost — you're just on the scenic route. And who knows? There might be a great coffee shop at the next turn.

Chapter 4: **The Ego's Costume Party**

(Masks, outfits, and the exhausting art of pretending you're fine.)

Beenie:

Sabine, sometimes I feel like my life has been one long costume party — only half the time, I didn't even pick my own outfit.

Sabine:

Oh, the Ego's Costume Party? Yeah, that's a classic. The ego loves costumes — the "I've got it all together" suit, the "I'm totally fine" mask, the "I'm happy for you" smile that hides just a pinch of "Why not me?" inside.

Beenie:

And you can't even leave early without making a scene. You just keep mingling, smiling, and hoping nobody notices that the mask is itchy and the shoes are killing you.

Why We Dress Up

The ego's main job is protection. It says, "If I wear this mask, they won't see me sweat. If I put on this costume, I'll fit in. If I play this role, I won't get hurt." And for a while, it works. You feel safe. You feel accepted. But eventually, you forget who you are without the mask — and that's when the costume starts wearing *you*.

Beenie:
So… it's like a bad wig you thought would be fun but now you can't get the thing off without yanking half your hair out?

Sabine:
Exactly. And the longer you wear it, the more tangled it gets.

Story Time

There was a season of my life where my ego was basically the host of the party. I wore the "Super Capable, Doesn't Need Help" costume like it was sewn into my skin. People thought I was confident, unstoppable — a real "Wow, she can do it all" kind of person.

Inside? I was exhausted. Lonely. I didn't want anyone to see the cracks because I thought they'd see weakness. So I smiled harder, worked longer, and nodded through conversations that had nothing to do with what I really wanted to say.

It was like standing in a crowded room, dressed as someone else, hoping somebody — anybody — would still recognize me.

Then one day, I realized: If I'm going to a costume party for the rest of my life, I at least want to be the one picking the outfit. Better yet, maybe I'll show up as... me. No mask. No itchy wig. Just me.

The Ego's Favorite Costumes

- **The Overachiever Cape:** "If I'm perfect, no one will criticize me."
- **The People-Pleaser Apron:** "If I make everyone happy, they'll love me."
- **The Lone Wolf Leather Jacket:** "If I don't need anyone, I can't be disappointed."
- **The Chameleon Hoodie:** "If I blend in, I won't stand out and risk judgment."

Beenie:

So basically, the ego's not evil — it's just a nervous stylist?

Sabine:

Exactly. It dresses you in whatever it thinks will keep you safe. But it's up to you to decide if that outfit still fits your life.

Unmasking Without Panic

Taking off your ego's costume doesn't have to be dramatic. You can start small:

- Speak up when you'd normally just smile and nod.
- Admit when you don't know something.
- Say "no" without adding a 10-minute apology.
- Let yourself be seen having a bad day without rushing to "fix" it.

Each little unmasking builds your confidence to show up as yourself.

Mini Wisdom Bombs

- *Your ego's mask is a survival tool — but it's not meant to be permanent.*
- *When you remove the costume, the people who truly love you won't flinch.*
- *You can't be loved for who you are if you're never showing who you are.*

Cat Corner 🐾

Gandalf: "Masks are silly. I always show my true self — usually on your pillow at 3 a.m."
Zafira: "If I wore a costume, it would be Queen of Everything. Because I already am."

Beenie's Dare

Today, notice one moment where you feel yourself putting on a "costume" to fit in or avoid judgment. Choose to leave it in the closet and show up as you instead.

Sabine's Brain Spark

The costume might win you applause, but only your true self will feel at home in your own skin.

25

Closing Wink

Life's too short for itchy wigs and shoes that pinch. If you're going to a party, go as yourself — you're the best character you've got.

Chapter 5: **Quantum Leap in Pajamas**

(Because you don't need to "look ready" to change your life.)

Beenie:

Sabine, I think the biggest scam we've all fallen for is the idea that you have to look the part before you take the leap.

Sabine:

Oh, 100%. Somewhere along the way, we were told you can't start until your hair's perfect, your ducks are in a row, and those ducks have matching outfits and synchronized swimming routines.

Beenie:

Which is hilarious, because the biggest life shifts I've ever made? I was in pajamas. Hair doing its own interpretive dance. Coffee stains optional but likely.

The Myth of "Looking Ready"

The world tells us:

- Get the degree first.
- Lose the weight first.
- Have the money saved first.
- Wait until the timing is right.

Meanwhile, life's just sitting there like, "Honey, you can leap in sweatpants if you want — the universe doesn't care what you're wearing."

Beenie:
So… the outfit's not the magic?

Sabine:
Nope. Action is the magic. Confidence comes from moving, not from waiting until you're dressed for the occasion.

Story Time

One of my biggest "quantum leap" moments didn't happen in a conference room or on a perfectly curated Instagram reel. It happened one morning at home. I was in my pajamas, hair in a "creative bun" (read: a mess), sipping coffee. And I realized — I could spend the next five years waiting until I looked and felt ready, or I could start now.

So I started. Still in pajamas. No "launch party," no approval from the peanut gallery. Just me, deciding I was done holding my own dreams hostage until they looked pretty.

The Science-y Bit

A "quantum leap" in physics is when something jumps from one state to another without traveling the distance in between. In life, it's when you skip all the "I'm not ready" steps and just... do it.

Does it feel weird? Yes. Will people question it? Absolutely. Will some of them clutch their pearls and tell you you're being reckless? Probably. But your life isn't a Broadway show — you don't need to wait for costume and makeup before stepping on stage.

Beenie:
So basically, leap first, lint-roll later?

Sabine:
Exactly. Action first, accessories later.

The Pajama Leap Playbook

1. **Say yes before you're ready.** (You'll figure it out as you go.)
2. **Start before you have all the details.** (The details reveal themselves in motion.)
3. **Ignore the peanut gallery.** (Especially the ones still ironing their "someday" outfit.)
4. **Celebrate starting messy.** (Because perfection is just a fancy word for procrastination.)

Mini Wisdom Bombs

- *Done in pajamas beats perfect in theory.*
- *If you wait until you "look ready," you'll wait forever.*
- *Your courage is more important than your outfit.*

Cat Corner 🐾

Gandalf: "I leap in pajamas all the time. They're called my fur."

Zafira: "If I waited until I was groomed to hunt the laser dot, I'd never get it."

Beenie's Dare

Think of one thing you've been putting off until you "look the part." Do it today — messy hair, pajamas, and all. Then celebrate like you just closed a million-dollar deal.

Sabine's Brain Spark

The leap isn't about being ready — it's about being willing.

Closing Wink

So the next time you think you can't take the leap because you're not dressed for it, remember: pajamas have witnessed some of the bravest decisions in history.

Chapter 6: **Cats Don't Apologize**

(Unapologetic self-worth, one paw at a time.)

Beenie:
Sabine, you ever notice cats never apologize?

Sabine:
All the time. They could knock over a glass, push your favorite mug off the counter, or walk across your laptop mid-Zoom call — and the closest thing you'll get to remorse is a slow blink.

Beenie:
Meanwhile, humans will apologize for *breathing too loudly* in a movie theater.

The Feline Confidence Factor

Cats walk through life like they own the place — because as far as they're concerned, they do. They don't ask for permission to take up space. They don't apologize for existing. And they *definitely* don't shrink themselves to make you comfortable.

Imagine what would happen if you lived like that — minus the hairball part.

Beenie:
So cats are basically tiny, fluffy life coaches?

Sabine:
Exactly. They're masters of unapologetic self-worth.

Story Time

Gandalf is still too little to leap onto the kitchen counter — but that hasn't stopped him from leaving his mark on my work. More than once, he's strolled across my keyboard mid-project like he's the co-author of this book.

The result? Entire paragraphs gone. Files closed without saving. Things I didn't even know a keyboard *could* do suddenly happening. And then… he looks right at me and starts purring. No apology. No hint of remorse. Just that "I own this place" energy wrapped in pure cuteness.

And honestly? There's a lesson in that. Gandalf didn't waste a second worrying if I'd be mad. He didn't shrink himself because he interrupted me. He just kept being his adorable, unapologetic self.

Why We Over-Apologize

Most of us were taught from a young age to smooth things over, to "be nice," to avoid rocking the boat. Somewhere along the way, apologizing became a reflex — not just for mistakes, but for being ourselves.

We say "sorry" for:

- Taking too long to text back.
- Asking for help.
- Saying no.
- Having needs.
- Taking up space in a room.

Cats? They'd never. They know their value is not up for debate.

Beenie:
Okay, but there's a difference between confidence and being a jerk, right?

Sabine:

Absolutely. Cats aren't malicious — they're just unapologetic. The trick is to hold your worth without trampling someone else's.

How to Channel Your Inner Cat

1. **Replace "sorry" with "thank you."**
   Instead of "Sorry I'm late," try "Thank you for waiting for me."
2. **Take up your space.**
   Sit, stand, and move like you belong — because you do.
3. **State your needs without apologizing for them.**
   "I need more time" is a complete sentence.
4. **Own your choices.**
   No nervous backpedaling required.

Mini Wisdom Bombs

- *Your value doesn't decrease because someone else doesn't see it.*
- *Apologies are for mistakes, not for existing.*
- *You teach people how to treat you by how you treat yourself.*

Cat Corner 🐾

Gandalf: "I've never once apologized for sitting on your keyboard. You're welcome for my input."

Zafira: "If you want an apology, you'll be waiting a long time. I suggest snacks instead."

Beenie's Dare

Today, catch yourself before you over-apologize. Swap it for a "thank you" or simply state your truth. Bonus points if you say it with cat-level confidence.

Sabine's Brain Spark

Confidence isn't about being louder — it's about standing in your worth without needing approval.

Closing Wink

So the next time you're tempted to apologize for something that isn't wrong, ask yourself: *What would a cat do?* Then slow blink, purr on the inside, and carry on.

Chapter 7: **The 3 AM Brain Circus**

(Because apparently, night is the perfect time to rethink every life choice you've ever made.)

Beenie:

Sabine, why is it that my brain waits until 3 a.m. — when it's dark, quiet, and I should be asleep — to hold a full-blown conference on everything I've ever done wrong since 1997?

Sabine:

Because your brain is secretly a night-shift carnival worker. Daytime? Closed for repairs. Middle of the night? Open for business — with flashing lights, loud music, and a clown juggling all your unresolved worries.

Beenie:

Exactly! It's like my mind says, "Oh good, you're finally still. Now, let's revisit that awkward conversation from 14 years ago and also plan for every possible disaster that may or may not happen in the next decade."

The Midnight Overthinker's Handbook

At 3 a.m., the brain is like a ringmaster introducing acts you never bought tickets for:

- The *What-If Tightrope Walker* — balancing worst-case scenarios like an Olympic sport.
- The *Past Regret Trapeze Artist* — swinging from "should have" to "could have" and back again.
- The *Lion Tamer of To-Do Lists* — because nothing says "bedtime" like remembering you still need to renew your driver's license.

Beenie:
So why does it happen at night?

Sabine:
Because you finally stop distracting yourself. During the day, you've got errands, conversations, and cat cuddles. At night, there's just you and the silence — and that's when the brain decides it's auditioning for Cirque du Overthink.

Story Time

One night, I woke up at exactly 3:12 a.m. with the sudden, urgent realization that I had never returned that VHS tape from the video store. You know — back when there were still *actual* video stores and rewinding your tape was considered good manners.

In my half-asleep panic, I imagined the late fees had been quietly compounding for years. By now, I probably owed them enough to buy the store, the strip mall it was in, and maybe the Blockbuster corporation itself.

For the next 30 minutes, I lay there wide-eyed, mentally preparing my apology speech for the store clerk who likely hadn't worked there since 2004.

By morning, I realized... the store had been closed for over a decade. My 3 a.m. panic was about as useful as a VHS tape without a VCR.

How to Tame the 3 a.m. Circus
1. **Get it out of your head.**
   Keep a notebook or your phone by the bed. Write it down so your brain knows it's "handled" for now.

2. **Do a body scan.**

   Shift focus from your thoughts to relaxing your toes, legs, hips, all the way up to your face.

3. **Name it, don't shame it.**

   Instead of "Ugh, I'm so stupid for overthinking," try "Okay, this is the part where my brain plays the late-night reruns."

4. **Use the Cat Method.**

   If a cat wouldn't lose sleep over it, maybe you shouldn't either.

Mini Wisdom Bombs

- *Your brain's job is to think. Your job is to decide which thoughts get the spotlight.*
- *Not every act in the circus deserves your attention.*
- *Night thoughts often look different under daylight.*

Cat Corner 🐾

Gandalf: "If I'm awake at 3 a.m., it's for important things — like chasing invisible ghosts."

Zafira: "If it's not about snacks or naps, it can wait until morning."

Beenie's Dare

Tonight, if you wake up to your own brain circus, don't engage with every act. Pick one calming focus — your breath, a happy memory, the sound of your cat purring — and let the rest pack up their tents.

Sabine's Brain Spark

Your 3 a.m. brain isn't wiser — it's just louder. Don't confuse volume with truth.

Closing Wink:

So next time the 3 a.m. circus rolls into town, remember — you don't have to buy a ticket. Just roll over, pull up the covers, and let the performers play to an empty house.

Chapter 8: **GPS Recalculating… Again**

(Because the plan is just a suggestion.)

Beenie:

Sabine, my GPS says "recalculating" like it's personally offended I didn't follow its perfect plan.

Sabine:

That's because it is. GPSs are control freaks. They map the "best route," and when you dare to take a different turn, they get passive-aggressive.

Beenie:

Which is kind of like life, isn't it? You set a plan, map it all out, and then something unexpected pops up — road closed, weather delay, or a sudden craving for pie — and suddenly, you're on a completely different road.

When the Map Changes

Life rarely goes exactly as planned. You get halfway to your goal and… boom:

- The job changes.
- The relationship shifts.
- The opportunity disappears.
- Your priorities evolve.

A recalculation isn't proof you failed — it's proof you're still moving.

Beenie:
So, the detour *isn't* the disaster?

Sabine:
Exactly. The detour is the part that teaches you the most — and sometimes it's the best part of the trip.

Story Time

I once had a route planned to meet a friend. Same town I'd been to before, so I figured, "I don't need GPS. I've got this."

Famous last words.

I took what I thought was the right exit and ended up deep in backroad country — no cell service, no landmarks, just winding roads and questionable cows staring me down.

At first, I was stressed about being late. But then I passed a lake so stunning I actually pulled over. A mile later, I found a farm stand selling fresh peaches. Then a little café with the best pie I've ever had in my life.

By the time I reached my friend, I was late — but I arrived with pie, peaches, and a way better story than if I'd just followed the original route.

Why Detours Feel So Hard
- We confuse "change" with "mistake."
- We're attached to the original timeline.
- We forget we're allowed to update our destination mid-trip.

How to Make Peace with Recalculation
1. **Pause before you panic.**
   Don't declare the trip ruined just because the road changed.
2. **Look for what's here now.**
   You might see something amazing you'd have missed otherwise.
3. **Let go of "should be."**
   Focus on *what is*.

4. **Collect souvenirs.**

    Physical or mental — something that marks the detour as worthwhile.

Mini Wisdom Bombs
- *The map is a guide, not a prison.*
- *You can arrive late and still arrive happy.*
- *Sometimes "wrong" turns take you exactly where you needed to go.*

Cat Corner 🐾

Gandalf: "I never take the same path twice. Keeps life interesting."

Zafira: "Sometimes the long way means more sunshine naps along the way."

Beenie's Dare

Think of one area of your life where you've been resisting change mid-route. This week, try leaning into the detour and see what unexpected "pie" shows up.

Sabine's Brain Spark

Recalculating isn't the GPS punishing you — it's the universe offering you a bonus round.

Closing Wink

So the next time life says "recalculating," just smile, turn up your favorite song, and take the scenic route. The pie is worth it.

Chapter 9: **The Gratitude Glitch**

(Why "just be grateful" sometimes feels fake — and how to make it real.)

Beenie:

Sabine, you know what phrase makes me want to throw a decorative pillow across the room?

Sabine:

"Live, laugh, love"?

Beenie:

That one's up there, but I was thinking "You should just be grateful."

Sabine:

Ah yes — the motivational equivalent of telling someone with a broken leg to "just walk it off."

When Gratitude Feels Fake

Gratitude is powerful — but when you're in a hard season, being told to "just be grateful" can feel dismissive. It skips over your very real feelings and replaces them with a forced smile.

That's what I call **The Gratitude Glitch** — when the practice of gratitude becomes a performance instead of something genuine.

Beenie:
So… it's not gratitude's fault, it's how we're told to use it?

Sabine:
Exactly. Gratitude is a tool, not a silencer. It should lift you up, not shut you down.

Story Time

Years ago, I was going through a rough patch. You know the kind — when even the "fun" things feel heavy and you're pretty sure your brain is running Windows 95. A well-meaning friend told me, "You should just be grateful, it could be worse."

And sure, it *could* have been worse, but that didn't magically make it feel better. I tried writing a gratitude list, but it read like a hostage note:

- I'm grateful for… coffee?
- My cat's cute?
- My socks match today?

None of it felt real because I was skipping the part where I admitted I was struggling. Once I let myself be honest — *"Life is tough right now and I'm grateful for the lesson... even if I have no idea what the lesson is yet"* — that's when gratitude started to feel authentic again.

The Gratitude Glitch Signs
- You feel guilty for having negative feelings.
- Your gratitude list feels flat or forced.
- You avoid talking about struggles because "I should just be thankful."
- Gratitude becomes something you "should" do, not something you feel.

How to Make Gratitude Real Again
1. **Start with honesty.**
   Acknowledge how you really feel before layering gratitude on top.
2. **Get specific.**
   "I'm grateful for my friend" is nice; "I'm grateful my friend called and made me laugh today" is richer.
3. **Mix the light and the heavy.**

Gratitude and challenges can coexist — it's not all-or-nothing.

4. **Make it physical.**
   Write it, speak it, or tell someone. Gratitude grows when shared.

Beenie:

So… it's not about being grateful for *everything* — it's about being grateful for something, even in the middle of everything?

Sabine:

Exactly. Gratitude isn't a denial of reality. It's a reminder that even in the hard, there's still good.

Mini Wisdom Bombs

- *Gratitude isn't pretending everything's fine — it's noticing the good while admitting what's hard.*
- *Real gratitude has roots in truth.*
- *You can be thankful and still want things to change.*

Cat Corner 🐾

Gandalf: "I'm grateful for snacks. Always snacks."

Zafira: "I'm grateful for naps… especially on your warm laundry."

Beenie's Dare

Today, write down three things you're grateful for — but add one honest detail about what's challenging right now. Let both truths exist on the same page.

Sabine's Brain Spark

Gratitude isn't a cover-up. It's a light switch you flip on to see what's still here, even in the dark.

Closing Wink:

So the next time someone says "just be grateful," smile and think, *I will — but on my terms.* Because the best gratitude is the kind that's real.

Chapter 10: **Sock Dimension, Part II: The Return of the Tupperware Lid**

(Some things do come back — and how to welcome them without resentment.)

Beenie:

Sabine, you remember the Sock Dimension?

Sabine:

How could I forget? The interdimensional vacation spot for missing socks, pens, and Tupperware lids.

Beenie:

Well... you're not going to believe this. One of my missing Tupperware lids just came back.

Sabine:

Seriously? Did it arrive by mail with a postcard from the Sock Dimension?

Beenie:

Close. It turned up in the back of the cupboard

behind a mixing bowl, like it had just decided to stroll home after years of "finding itself."

When the Missing Returns

Life has a funny way of circling things back to you — a person, an opportunity, a dream you thought you'd put away for good. Sometimes it's exactly what you wanted. Sometimes it's… a Tupperware lid you're not even sure you still own the matching container for.

The trick? Deciding whether to welcome it back or let it go again without guilt.

Beenie:
So, it's not always "Yay, you're back!" — sometimes it's "Oh… you again."

Sabine:
Exactly. Not everything that returns is meant to stay.

Story Time

Years ago, I had a friendship fade out. No drama, just life doing its thing. Then one day, out of the blue, they popped back into my life. At first, it was like finding that missing lid — "Oh, hey, where have you been?" But as we reconnected, I realized the person who came back wasn't the same as the one who left.

And neither was I.

We still cared about each other, but the "container" — the context for our friendship — didn't quite fit anymore. That didn't mean the return was bad. It just meant it served a different purpose now — like a lid that works best on a new container you didn't even have back when it first disappeared.

Why Returns Can Feel Tricky
- You've changed, they've changed.
- Nostalgia clouds your judgment.
- You feel obligated to make it fit again.
- You're afraid of "wasting" the chance.

How to Handle the Return of the Lid
1. **Check the fit.** Does this still work for who you are now?
2. **Release the guilt.** Letting it go again isn't failure.

3. **Repurpose it.** Maybe it fits into your life differently this time.
4. **Celebrate the story.** Even if it's just a quick hello before parting ways again.

Mini Wisdom Bombs

- *Not everything that comes back is meant to stay.*
- *Sometimes closure arrives in the form of a return visit.*
- *You can appreciate the return without forcing it to fit.*

Cat Corner 🐾

Gandalf: "If a toy comes back after I've lost it, I assume it's a gift from the universe."
Zafira: "If it's not food, it better at least be shiny."

Beenie's Dare

Think of one thing (or person) that's reappeared in your life lately. Ask yourself: Does this still fit who I am now? If not, let it go with gratitude.

Sabine's Brain Spark

When something returns, it's an invitation — not an obligation.

Closing Wink

So the next time a "Tupperware lid" wanders back into your life, check if it still has a container. If it does, great. If it doesn't, thank it for the reunion — and set it free back to the Sock Dimension.

Chapter 11: **Laser Pointer Goals**

(How to focus without chasing every shiny distraction.)

Beenie:

Sabine, I think I finally understand what my problem is with focus.

Sabine:

Do tell.

Beenie:

It's basically the same as Zafira and Gandalf with the laser pointer. I'll be laser-focused... and then something else shiny comes along and suddenly I'm halfway across the room wondering what I was doing.

Sabine:

Ah yes, the *Laser Pointer Syndrome*. One minute you're locked in, the next you're chasing an idea that feels urgent but is actually just... shiny.

The Illusion of the Laser Dot

The laser dot isn't real — you can't actually catch it. And yet, it feels *so* worth the chase in the moment. Life has its own laser pointers:

- The "new" idea that's way more exciting than the hard work you're doing now.
- The opportunity that sounds amazing but pulls you off course.
- The random project you convince yourself is *essential* right this second.

Beenie:
So… you're saying not every shiny thing is worth chasing?

Sabine:
Exactly. Some are distractions disguised as opportunities. The trick is knowing which is which.

Story Time

A while back, I was deep into a project I really cared about. But then — bam! — a new idea popped into my head. It was *good*, it was exciting, and it felt way more fun than slogging through the hard part of what I was already working on.

So I put my main project on pause to chase the "laser dot." Weeks later, the dot was gone, the thrill had faded, and my original project was gathering dust.

I realized I'd been tricked by momentum that wasn't leading anywhere.

How to Tell if It's a Goal or a Laser Dot
1. **Does it align with your big-picture vision?**
2. **Will it still matter in six months?**
3. **Does it build on what you've already started?**
4. **Are you chasing it to avoid the hard part of something else?**

If you answered "no" to the first three and "yes" to the last one… congratulations, you've got yourself a laser dot.

Beenie:
So if it's a laser dot, what do I do?

Sabine:

You make a note of it — then you go back to your main goal. If it's still exciting later, revisit it. If not, it was never worth the chase.

Mini Wisdom Bombs

- *Not every shiny thing is progress.*
- *Discipline is chasing one dot until you catch it.*
- *The thrill of the chase fades faster than you think.*

Cat Corner 🐾

Gandalf: "Every dot is worth chasing. I regret nothing."
Zafira: "I only chase the dots that come with treats."

Beenie's Dare

Pick one goal you've been tempted to abandon for something "shiny." Commit to sticking with it for the next 30 days, no matter what other dots appear.

Sabine's Brain Spark

Focus isn't about ignoring every distraction — it's about knowing which chases are worth the run.

Closing Wink

So the next time life waves a laser pointer at you, pause. Make sure it's a real goal, not just a flashy distraction — unless, of course, it comes with pie.

Chapter 12: **The Universal Lost & Found**

(Trusting that what's truly yours will find its way back.)

Beenie:

Sabine, do you believe in the whole "If it's meant to be, it'll come back" thing?

Sabine:

You mean the cosmic equivalent of the Lost & Found box? Yeah — though sometimes it feels less like "meant to be" and more like "Why are you back in my life, and what am I supposed to do with you?"

Beenie:

Exactly! Some things return like long-lost friends. Others… show up like that hoodie from your ex that you forgot you had — and you're not sure if you should wear it or burn it.

The Cosmic Lost & Found Department

The universe has this uncanny way of returning things — people, dreams, opportunities — when you least expect it.

- The job you didn't get, but later a better version of it appears.
- The friend you lost touch with, who messages you out of the blue.
- The skill you shelved years ago, suddenly relevant again.

Beenie:
But how do you know if something's worth keeping the second time around?

Sabine:
Simple — you ask, "Does this still fit who I am now?" If yes, keep it. If no, send it back to the cosmic bin.

Story Time

I once dreamed about starting a specific project — but at the time, I didn't have the resources, connections, or even the confidence to do it. I shelved the idea.

Years later, out of nowhere, the perfect conditions appeared: the right people, timing, and tools. It was like the universe had been holding it in storage, waiting for me to be ready.

If it had come back earlier, I wouldn't have been able to do it justice. But when it returned at the right time? I was ready, and it fit perfectly.

Why Things Come Back
- You're finally ready for them.
- The timing now supports their success.
- You've grown into the person who can handle them.

How to Handle a Return from the Universal Lost & Found
1. **Check the fit.** Does it align with your life now?
2. **Ask why now?** Timing matters.
3. **Decide with intention.** Keep it or release it — no guilt.
4. **Be open to surprises.** Sometimes what returns is better than what you lost.

Mini Wisdom Bombs

- *If it's truly yours, it'll find its way back.*
- *Not everything that returns is meant to stay.*
- *The right timing can turn an old "no" into a perfect "yes."*

Cat Corner 🐾

Gandalf: "If I lose a toy, I trust you'll find it. Preferably before nap time."
Zafira: "If it's meant for me, it'll show up in my food bowl."

Beenie's Dare

Think of something that's returned to you recently — a person, idea, or opportunity. Instead of reacting automatically, pause and ask: Does this fit who I am today?

Sabine's Brain Spark

What's meant for you won't need chasing — it will arrive and feel like it belongs.

Closing Wink

So the next time something pops up from your personal Lost & Found, don't just toss it back in the drawer. Check if it still has a place in your life — and if it does, welcome it home.

Chapter 13: **Cat Wisdom for Humans**

(Eat, nap, stretch, repeat — the underrated self-care plan.)

Beenie:

Sabine, I swear cats have this whole life thing figured out better than we do.

Sabine:

Of course they do. They're basically furry little Zen masters — with just a dash of chaos.

Beenie:

Exactly! They eat when they're hungry, nap when they're tired, play when they feel like it, and have no problem setting boundaries. Meanwhile, humans will skip lunch, push through exhaustion, and say yes when we want to scream "Nope!"

Lesson 1: Prioritize Rest

Cats never apologize for napping. They don't feel guilty for recharging. Gandalf can go from 100 mph zoomies to full nap mode in under 60 seconds — and he doesn't once think, "I really should be more productive right now."

Takeaway: Rest isn't a reward for burning out — it's maintenance for staying awesome.

Lesson 2: Ask for What You Want

Zafira doesn't hint when she wants attention — she plants herself in front of me, locks eyes, and meows until I get the message. Cats are masters of direct communication.

Takeaway: Don't drop vague hints and hope people get it. Ask clearly.

Lesson 3: Stretch Often

Every time a cat gets up from a nap, they stretch like they're greeting the day for the first time. That simple act keeps them limber and ready to pounce.

Takeaway: Move your body often — not just at the gym. Stretching resets your energy.

Lesson 4: Own Your Space

Gandalf doesn't hesitate to claim the best spot in the house — even if it's the exact moment I need that spot. Cats act like they belong everywhere they go.

Takeaway: Stop shrinking yourself to fit in. Claim your space, physically and metaphorically.

Story Time

One day, I was watching Zafira sprawled across my desk like she owned it — head high, eyes half-closed, radiating queen energy. And it hit me: she's not worried about who thinks she should sit somewhere else. She's not waiting for an invitation. Meanwhile, I've caught myself hesitating to step into places or situations because I wasn't "sure I belonged." Cats don't wrestle with that. They decide they belong — and so they do.

Lesson 5: Play Every Day

Even older cats still chase toys or stalk imaginary prey. Play isn't just for kittens — it's for life.

Takeaway: Make space for joy, silliness, and hobbies that have no productivity goal.

Mini Wisdom Bombs

- *Rest is essential, not optional.*
- *Ask directly for what you need.*
- *Movement keeps you ready for opportunity.*
- *Own your space.*
- *Play keeps you alive inside.*

Cat Corner 🐾

Gandalf: "My secret? Nap like you mean it."
Zafira: "If you want something, claim it. Humans overcomplicate things."

Beenie's Dare

Today, pick one "cat habit" and practice it: nap without guilt, ask clearly for something, stretch like you're on a yoga retreat, or claim your space.

Sabine's Brain Spark

Sometimes the best life advice doesn't come from a guru — it comes with whiskers and a tail.

Closing Wink:

So next time you wonder what to do, just ask yourself: *What would a cat do?* Then do it — with style.

Chapter 14: **The Cosmic Customer Service Line**

(Manifesting is just placing an order… without micromanaging delivery.)

Beenie:

Sabine, sometimes I feel like manifesting is calling cosmic customer service — you put in your request, but then you want to call back every five minutes to see if they're working on it.

Sabine:

Exactly. And the universe is over there, headset on, saying, "Ma'am, your order is in the system. Please stop hovering over my shoulder."

Beenie:

I mean… I just want to be sure they *got it*.

Sabine:

Oh, they got it. The problem is when you start "tracking" your manifestation like a package and then panicking when it doesn't update every 30 seconds.

How the Cosmic Order Works

1. **Clarity:** You decide what you want.
2. **Request:** You put it out there — in words, vision boards, prayers, whatever works for you.
3. **Alignment:** You live in a way that matches your order.
4. **Trust:** You let the universe handle the *how* and *when*.

Beenie:

So... why is the trust part so hard?

Sabine:

Because humans love control. You think if you check the oven every two minutes, the cake will bake faster — but really, you're just letting the heat out.

Story Time

For about two decades, I had this dream — starting a foundation that would make a real difference for people in a big way. The kind of thing that changes lives, lifts burdens, and leaves people breathing easier.

But for years, I didn't act on it. I had no clue where to start, what to do, or even exactly how I'd serve. So the dream just stayed... well, dreamy.

Then one day, a post popped up on Facebook that lit the fuse. Something in me just said, *This is it. Move now.* Within days, I had the idea mapped out. Within weeks, we had a name, a mission, and the paperwork in motion. And before I could catch my breath, the Happiness Matters Foundation was a living, breathing thing — out in the world, doing exactly what I'd always dreamed of.

That dream didn't come to life because I micromanaged the universe. It showed up when the timing, inspiration, and readiness aligned — and all I had to do was say "Yes" when the door opened.

Signs You're Micromanaging Your Manifestation
- Constantly asking "When will it happen?"
- Changing your order every few days.
- Trying to control every step of the process.
- Feeling like you need to "earn" it in exhausting ways.

How to Let the Universe Do Its Job

1. **Place your order once — clearly.**
2. **Live as if it's already on its way.**
3. **Take inspired action** (but don't force it).
4. **Release the timeline.**

Mini Wisdom Bombs

- *Trust is part of the order.*
- *If you keep changing your request, the universe can't deliver.*
- *Your job is the "what," not the "how."*

Cat Corner 🐾

Gandalf: "I ask for treats once. Then I nap until they appear."

Zafira: "I never wonder *when* dinner is coming — I just know it will."

Beenie's Dare

Think of one thing you've been over-checking with the universe. Write it down, declare it done, and then focus on living in alignment — without "calling back."

Sabine's Brain Spark

The universe isn't ignoring you — it's working behind the scenes. Give it space to deliver.

Closing Wink

So the next time you place your cosmic order, hang up the phone and go live your life. Your "package" is on the way — no tracking number required.

Chapter 15: **The Art of the Strategic Nope**

(Why "No" can be the most loving word you say — for yourself and others.)

Beenie:
Sabine, I've decided "No" is my new self-care routine.

Sabine:
Congratulations — you've just unlocked Level 7 Adulting.

Beenie:
Seriously though, I used to say yes to everything. Yes to extra work. Yes to events I didn't want to attend. Yes to "quick favors" that were neither quick nor favors. I was basically the "Free Samples" table at Costco — available, accessible, and a little exhausted.

Why 'No' is a Yes to You

Every time you say no to something that drains you, you're saying yes to:

- Your time.
- Your energy.
- Your mental and emotional health.

"No" is not rejection — it's redirection.

Sabine:

Think of it like pruning a plant. You're not being mean; you're making space for healthier growth.

Story Time

A few years ago, I started to *really* understand the value of "no."

Back then, I was still in the habit of saying yes to things I didn't want to do — projects, events, "quick favors" that somehow ate up hours of my life. One day, I said yes to helping with something I had zero interest in because I didn't want to disappoint anyone.

Three weeks later, I was annoyed, exhausted, and mentally composing my resignation letter while smiling politely. Finally, it hit me: *Why am I still here?*

So I said no. Politely, firmly, and without over-explaining. And here's the thing — the world didn't collapse, nobody burst into tears, and they found someone who actually wanted the role. Meanwhile, I got my time, energy, and peace back. That was the moment I realized "no" isn't mean — it's freedom.

The Strategic Nope Formula

1. **Pause** — Don't answer right away.
2. **Check alignment** — Does this light you up or wear you down?
3. **Answer with kindness** — "Thanks for thinking of me, but I'll have to pass."
4. **Stick to it** — No backpedaling, no over-explaining.

Mini Wisdom Bombs

- *Every "yes" is also a "no" to something else.*
- *If it's not a "heck yes," it's probably a no.*
- *You're allowed to protect your peace.*

Cat Corner 🐾

Gandalf: "If I don't want to be petted, I just walk away. No guilt, no explanation."

Zafira: "I've been saying 'no' to cheap kibble since day one. Standards, darling."

Beenie's Dare

Pick one thing this week to say "no" to — big or small — and notice how freeing it feels.

Sabine's Brain Spark

Boundaries aren't walls; they're doors you choose to open or close.

Closing Wink

So go ahead — serve a well-brewed "No" with a smile. The people who matter will respect it, and the rest? Well, they'll find another coffee shop.

Chapter 16: **The Last Cup in the Pot**

(Savoring the ending before starting something new.)

Beenie:

You know, Sabine, the last cup of coffee in the pot is always the most... complicated.

Sabine:

Complicated? It's coffee. Either drink it or don't.

Beenie:

Oh no — the last cup has layers. Sometimes it's the perfect strength. Sometimes it's a bitter sludge of coffee grounds and regret. But it's also your final sip before deciding, "Do I make a fresh pot or call it a day?"

Why the Last Cup Matters

The last cup is the moment before a transition — an ending before the next beginning. It forces you to pause and decide:

- Am I satisfied?
- Do I need more?
- Is it time to switch to tea?

We do this in life, too. We cling to the "last cup" of relationships, jobs, habits, or chapters because we're unsure if we're ready to brew something new.

Beenie:
So… sometimes you sip it slowly to savor it. Other times you just toss it and move on.

Sabine:
Exactly. Endings don't have to be dramatic. They can be a gentle acknowledgment that this pot — or season of life — is finished.

Story Time

When I left my mortgage loan officer career (which was neither my dream nor my happy place), it felt like pouring out the last cold cup in the pot. I'd been sipping on that job for too long, hoping it would taste better with time. Spoiler: it didn't.

The morning of April 1, 2018, I looked at my metaphorical coffee mug and thought, *Oh, this is stupid. Why am I drinking this? I'm miserable.* So I stopped. No grand plan, no safety net — just the certainty that it was time to brew something new. That choice eventually led me here, doing work that lights me up every day.

How to Know When It's the Last Cup
- You're drinking it out of habit, not joy.
- You keep hoping it'll magically taste better.
- You're avoiding brewing something new because it's "work."

What to Do with the Last Cup
1. **Acknowledge it.** Say, "This season is ending."
2. **Decide if you'll savor it or toss it.**
3. **Clear the pot.** Make room for what's next.

Mini Wisdom Bombs

- *Not all endings are bad — some are just overdue.*
- *You can't pour new coffee into a full pot.*
- *The last sip can be the start of something better.*

Cat Corner 🐾

Gandalf: "When the bowl's empty, I don't mourn — I meow for more."

Zafira: "If the pot's empty, stop staring at it and get someone else to make more. Queens don't pour their own coffee."

Beenie's Dare

Identify one "last cup" in your life right now — something you've been holding onto that's ready to end. Decide whether to savor it, release it, or make something fresh.

Sabine's Brain Spark

The last cup isn't the end of coffee — it's the invitation to brew again, this time exactly how you like it.

Closing Wink

So here's to the last cup — may you know when to savor it, when to pour it out, and when to brew something even better.

Chapter 17: **And Another Thing…**

(Because endings are really just beginnings in disguise.)

Beenie:

So… this is it. The end of the book.

Sabine:

End? Nah. This is just where we hand the keys over to the reader. We've been the GPS, but now it's their turn to actually drive.

Beenie:

Which means they can take the scenic route, blast their own playlist, and ignore your "recalculating" voice if they want to.

Sabine:

Rude, but accurate.

The Point of It All

If you've made it this far, you've probably noticed something — this wasn't about giving you a neat little list of "Ten Steps to Perfect Happiness" (because… ew). It's about you seeing how ridiculously capable you already are.

We've talked about coffee, cats, and saying no. We've gotten real about endings, beginnings, and that messy middle part where you want to quit but know you shouldn't. And if you remember nothing else, remember this:

Sabine:
You've already survived 100% of your hardest days. You're not fragile glass — you're a disco ball. You don't break, you just reflect the light differently.

Beenie:
Ooh, that's good. Can we put that on a mug?

Sabine:
Only if it's dishwasher safe.

What Happens Next

Here's the secret no one tells you — there's no "next level" you have to earn before you're allowed to enjoy life. You don't need to be more enlightened, more successful, or more "ready" before you start doing the things that light you up.

The only thing you need? To start. Messy, imperfect, gloriously human starting.

Cat Corner 🐾

Gandalf: "The key to happiness? Nap when you need to, play when you want to, and don't overthink the empty bowl — it will get filled."
Zafira: "Life's too short for bad kibble, boring naps, or people who don't adore you. Carry on."

Beenie's Final Dare

Before you close this book, write down one thing you're going to do differently starting today. Not next week. Not "someday." Today. Then do it — even if it's tiny. Especially if it's tiny.

Sabine's Brain Spark

Life doesn't hand out report cards for how "well" you lived it. It's about the moments you made matter — to yourself and to others.

Final Wink

So go on, take your stories, your sass, your spark, and make something wonderful. And when you forget how, remember we've been here before — and you've always found your way back to joy.

About the Author

Beenie Mann is a perspective-shifter, hope-sparker, and unapologetic coffee enthusiast who believes life doesn't have to be perfect to be worth loving. As the founder of *Matters of Perspective®* and the *Happiness Matters Foundation*, she helps people rediscover their spark, shift their thinking, and create lives they love — one conversation (and one cup of coffee) at a time.

A certified Quantum Healing Hypnosis Technique® (QHHT) practitioner, PSYCH-K® facilitator, and creator of the "Stupid Simple" courses, Beenie's work blends practical tools, soulful insight, and just enough sass to keep things real. Whether through books, workshops, or her online community, she's on a mission to remind people that hope, happiness, and change are always possible — even when life feels like it's run out of creamer.

When she's not writing, teaching, or guiding transformational sessions, you can find Beenie at home in Colorado with her husband and their two delightfully mischievous cats, Gandalf and Zafira, and a coffee mug that's rarely empty.

Follow Beenie:

Website – MattersOfPerspective.com

Foundation – HappinessMattersFoundation.org

Facebook - https://www.facebook.com/mattersofperspective/

Twitter - https://twitter.com/beenie_mann

LinkedIn - https://www.linkedin.com/in/mattersofperspective/

Author Page on Amazon – www.beeniemann.com

Made in United States
Troutdale, OR
08/11/2025